Centre for Baptist History an
Occasional Papers Volume 21 an

The Whitley Lecture 2022

# The Ruling Christ and the Witnessing Church:
## Towards a Baptist Political Theology

Centre for Baptist History and Heritage Studies
Occasional Papers Volume 21 and Whitley Publications

The Whitley Lecture 2022

# The Ruling Christ and the Witnessing Church:
## Towards a Baptist Political Theology

Andy Goodliff

**Regent's Park College, Oxford**

Regent's Park College is a Permanent Private Hall of The University of Oxford.

Copyright ©Andy Goodliff 2022

First published 2022

Centre for Baptist Studies,
Regent's Park College,
Pusey Street,
Oxford,
OX1 2LB
(Regent's Park College is a Permanent Private Hall of
the University of Oxford.)
www.rpc.ox.ac.uk

19 18 17 16 15 14 13    7 6 5 4 3 2 1

The right of Andy Goodliff to be identified as the Author of
this Work has been asserted by him in accordance with the
Copyright, Designs and Patents Act 1988

*All rights reserved. No part of this publication may be reproduced, stored
in a retrieval system, or transmitted in any form or by any means,
electric, mechanical, photocopying, recording or otherwise, without the
prior permission of the publisher or a license permitting restricted
copying. In the UK such licenses are issued by the Copyright Licensing
Agency, 90 Tottenham Court Road, London W1P 9HE.*

British Library Cataloguing in Publication Data
A catalogue record for this book is available from the British Library

ISBN 9798779073158

Front Cover Illustration: 'Burnt copy of John Bunyan's *The Pilgrim's Progress* (1688),
from The Angus Library, Regent'Park College, Oxford.
Back cover illustration by Chris Lewis. Used with permission.

Typeset by Larry J. Kreitzer

# The Whitley Lectures

Nigel G. Wright, *Power and Discipleship: Towards a Baptist Theology of the State* (1996-97)

Ruth M.B. Gouldbourne, *Reinventing the Wheel: Women and Ministry in English Baptist Life* (1997-98)

Keith G. Jones, *A Shared Meal and a Common Table: Some Reflections on the Lord's Supper and Baptists* (1999)

Anne Dunkley, *Seen and Heard: Reflections on Children and Baptist Tradition* (1999-2000)

Stephen Finamore, *Violence, the Bible and the End of the World* (2001)

Nicholas J. Wood, *Confessing Christ in a Plural World* (2002)

Stephen R. Holmes, *Tradition and Renewal in Baptist Life* (2003)

Andrew Rollinson, *Liberating Ecclesiology: Setting the Church Free to Live Out its Missionary Nature* (2004)

Kate Coleman, *Being Human: A Black British Christian Woman's Perspective* (2006)

Sean Winter, *More Light and Truth?: Biblical Interpretation in Covenantal Perspective* (2007)

Craig Gardiner, *How can we sing the Lord's Song?: Worship in and out of the Church* (2008)

Sally Nelson, *A Thousand Crucifixions: The Materialist Subversion of the Church?* (2009)

David Southall, *The Poetic Paul: On Creating New Realities for Righteousness in Romans* (2010)

E. Anne Clements, *Wrestling with the Word: A Woman reads Scripture* (2011)

Ian M. Randall, *Religious Liberty in Continental Europe: Campaigning by British Baptists, 1840s to 1930s* (2012)

Michael J. Peat, *Answering Mendel's Dwarf: Thinking Theologically about Genetic Selection* (2013)

Helen J. Dare, *Always on the way and in the fray: Reading the Bible as Baptists* (2014)

Ed Kaneen, *What is Biblical 'Ministry'?: Revisiting* diakonia *in the New Testament* (2015)

Joshua T. Searle, *Church Without Walls: Post-Soviet Baptists After the Ukrainian Revolution, 2013–14* (2016)

Richard Pollard, *The Pioneering Evangelicalism of Dan Taylor (1738-1816)* (2017)

Helen Paynter, *Dead and Buried? Attending to the voices of the victim in the Old Testament and Today: Towards an ethical reading of the Old Testament texts of violence* (2018)

Joe Kapolyo, *Theology and Culture: An Afrucan Perspective* (2019)

Robert Parkinson, *Finding A Friend: The Baptist Encounter with Judaism* (2020)

David McLachlan, *Does This Cross Have Disabled Access? Re-thinking Theologies of Atonement and Disability* (2021)

Andy Goodliff, *The Ruling Christ and the Witnessing Church: Towards a Baptist Political Theology* (2022)

# The Whitley Lecture

The Whitley Lecture was first established in 1949 in honour of W.T. Whitley (1861–1947), the Baptist minister and historian. Following a pastorate in Bridlington, during which he also taught at Rawdon College in Yorkshire, Whitley became the first Principal of the Baptist College of Victoria in Melbourne, Australia, in 1891. This institution was later renamed Whitley College in his honour.

Whitley was a key figure in the formation of the Baptist Historical Society in 1908. He edited its journal, which soon gained an international reputation for the quality of its contents – a reputation it still enjoys nearly a century later as the *Baptist Quarterly*. His *A History of British Baptists* (London: Charles Griffin, 1923) remains an important source of information and comment for contemporary historians. Altogether he made an important contribution to Baptist life and self understanding in Britain and Australia, providing a model of how a pastor-scholar might enrich the life and faith of others.

The establishment of the annual lecture in his name is designed as an encouragement to research and writing by Baptist scholars, and to enable the results of this work to be published. The giving of grants, advice and other forms of support by the Lectureship Committee serves the same purpose. The committee consists of representatives of the British Baptist Colleges, the Baptist Union of Great Britain, BMS World Mission, the Baptist Ministers' Fellowship and the Baptist Historical Society. These organizations also provide financial support for its work.

In this Lecture, Andy Goodliff offers us a crafted exploration of what a Baptist political theology might be. His argument begins with an overview of Nigel Wright's discussion of church and state but soon moves into a powerful reflection upon what it means today to inhabit a dissenting ecclesiology, one which says 'no' to the power of the state and 'yes' to the Lordship of Christ. To be baptised is a political act; to accede to the Declaration of Principle implies a political worldview; to be a member of a Baptist church commits us to an ongoing 'political discipleship' in which we constantly engage in reflective conversation with the powers around us. This is a Lecture to stimulate both our thinking and our dissent.

Andy Goodliff has been the minister of Belle Vue Baptist Church, Southend-on-Sea since 2010. He studied for a BA in Theology at King's College London (2003), followed by an MA in Youth Ministry (2004) also at King's. He then spent several years as a church youth worker and RE teacher before training for ministry at Regent's Park College, Oxford and reading for an MTh in Applied Theology (2010). He completed a PhD at St. Andrew's in 2018, which has since been published as *Renewing a Modern Denomination* (Pickwick, 2020). He has co-edited *Gathering Disciples* (2017), *Rhythms of Faithfulness* (2018) and *Reconciling Rites* (2020), and is a co-founder of Theology Live and an editor of the *Journal of Baptist Theology in Context*. Andy is married to Hannah and they have three children.

Sally Nelson, Secretary to the Whitley Trust Committee

# The Ruling Christ snd the Witnessing Church:
## Towards a Baptist Political Theology

### Andy Goodliff

What might a Baptist political theology look like? Twenty-five years ago Nigel Wright gave the first Lecture in a new series of Whitley Lectures. It was called *Power and Discipleship: Towards a Baptist Theology of the State* and drew on the argument of his 1994 PhD *Disavowing Constantine*, which was a study of mission, church and state in the theologies of John Howard Yoder and Jürgen Moltmann.[1] Wright has been something of a lone voice amongst Baptists to attempt to articulate a Baptist theological engagement with politics.[2] While Baptists have learned much from and have followed substantially

---

[1] Wright's thesis was published by Paternoster in 2000 under the same name. The front cover includes the words 'A Radical Baptist Perspective on Church, Society and State.' *Free Church, Free State: A Positive Baptist Vision* (Milton Keynes: Paternoster, 2005) was a more accessible version of the same argument.

[2] Alongside *Power and Discipleship* (Oxford: Whitley, 1996), *Disavowing Constantine* (Carlisle: Paternoster, 2000) and *Free Church, Free,* see also, 'Called to Non-conform' in *Challenge to Change* (Kingsway, 1991); 'Disestablishment: A Contemporary View from the Free Churches', *Anvil* 12:2 (1995): 121-35; 'Radical Politics' in *The Radical Evangelical* (London: SPCK, 1996), 103-19; 'Church and Society: Shifting Paradigms' in *New Baptists, New Agenda* (Carlisle: Paternoster, 2002), 96-111; and 'Government as Ambiguous Power' in Nick Spencer and Jonathan Chaplin (eds.), *God and Government* (London: SPCK, 2009); and 'Humane religion: evangelical faith, Baptist identity, and liberal secularism' in *Beyond 400: Exploring Baptist Futures* edited by David J. Cohen and Michael Parsons (Eugene, OR: Pickwick, 2011), 17-33.

Wright's wider theological vision for Baptist life, his main theological interest in political theology has largely been ignored.[3]

I want to begin this lecture by exploring the reason for its subject matter. First, it is a return to issues that Nigel Wright's Whitley Lecture addressed, but from a different starting point.[4] It seems overdue to revisit the question of Baptists and politics,[5] distinguishing as Wright did, between Baptist and Anabaptist.[6] Second, it came from reading Luke Bretherton's magisterial introduction to political theology, *Christ and the Common Life*. His chapters on Pentecostalism, Catholic Social Teaching and Anglicanism raised the question of what a chapter on a Baptist political theology might say.[7] This is a brief attempt to sketch out some possibilities. Third, it is a reflection that recently it has been difficult for any of us to be uninterested, or at least, unaware of politics.

---

[3] See Andy Goodliff, 'Nigel Wright's Radical Baptist Theology', *Baptist Quarterly* 48.2 (April 2017), 69-77.

[4] See chapter one of Luke Bretherton, *Christianity and Contemporary Politics* (Oxford: Wiley-Blackwell, 2010), which argues for changing patterns between church and state from the 1990s onwards.

[5] Of course other Whitley Lectures have been concerned with politics with regards to gender, race, disability, as well the politics of reading the Bible, celebrating the Eucharist and worshipping God. Politics should not be reduced to what happens at an election or in Parliament.

[6] Works exploring an Anabaptist political theology have been increasing in the last half-century, initiated by John Howard Yoder (although his reputation is now seriously questioned following persistent sexual misconduct). The second edition of *Wiley Blackwell Companion to Political Theology* (Oxford: Wiley-Blackwell, 2018) has a chapter on 'Anabaptist Political Theologies', but there is no chapter and only one reference in the whole book to a Baptist perspective. Baptists are mentioned along with other dissenters by Elaine Graham on her chapter on feminist theology as those who helped break the mould of male leadership.

[7] An earlier prompt came from a line in a paper given by Brian Haymes in 2009 that said 'we urgently need more work at unashamedly political theologies', which has stayed with me.

In Britain, since 2010, there have been four General Elections,[8] three referendums,[9] and in addition, the events of the Windrush Scandal, the Grenfell Fire, the #MeToo and Black Lives Matter movements, and of course Brexit, the COVID pandemic, and the climate emergency, all raising questions of politics. Politics dominates our lives. At the same time there have been some who are seeking to articulate, from what we call the Left and the Right, and within the Church of England, a political vision and narrative for the times.[10] It therefore seems appropriate, necessary even, for Baptists to be engaging in the task of political theology.

**What is Political Theology?**

What does it mean to speak of political theology?[11] It might be assumed that political theology is the engagement of theology with questions and issues of politics (the ordering and structures of society), most notably that of the relationship between church and state. Luke Bretherton begins with a definition of 'politics' that he connects with a 'good or

---

[8] 2010, 2015, 2017 and 2019.

[9] Alternative Vote (2011), Scottish independence (2014) and European Union Membership (2016).

[10] For example, Philip Blond, *Red Tory* (London: Faber & Faber, 2010); Ian Geary and Adrian Pabst (eds.), *Blue Labour: Forging a New Politics* (London: I. B. Tauris, 2015); Nicholas Sagovsky and Peter McGrail (eds.), *Together for the Common Good* (London: SCM, 2015); Justin Welby, *Reimagining Britain* (London: Bloomsbury, 2018); Jonathan Chaplin and Andrew Bradstock, *The Future of Brexit Britain: Anglican Reflections on National Identity and European Solidarity* (London: SPCK, 2020).

[11] I am following Bretherton here, but see also Elizabeth Philips, *Political Theology: A Guide for the Perplexed* (London: T & T Clark, 2012); Peter Scott and William T. Cavanaugh (eds.), *The Wiley-Blackwell Companion to Political Theology* (Wiley-Blackwell, 2018[2]); Craig Hovey and Elizabeth Philips (eds.), *The Cambridge Companion to Christian Political Theology* (Cambridge : Cambridge University Press, 2015).

flourishing life' that is always 'embedded in some form of common life' because we are social creatures.[12] Politics, then, is what determines whether that common life is flourishing, that is, whether it is 'just or unjust, generous or heartless, peaceable or violent.'[13] Theological politics has its starting point with Jesus and 'the meaning, purpose, and ordering of human life in response to the revelation of God given in Jesus.'[14] The claim 'Jesus is Lord' means theology 'always has a political valence.'[15] Political theology, according to Bretherton, 'discerns the consonance and dissonance between the form of rule incarnated and inaugurated by Jesus Christ and the orders and authorities shaping this age between Christ's ascension and return.'[16] Political theology is not one thing, but has 'multiple pathways,' shaped by ecclesial traditions, movements or philosophies.[17] Some have discerned two streams: political theology is focused on the politics of the world, and how salvation is to do with the political, economic, and social; whereas theological politics articulates how the church has its own politics.[18]

The church does not have an option to whether it engages with politics, it is an unavoidable part of acknowledging the Lordship of Jesus.

---

[12] Bretherton, *Christ and the Common Life*, 17.
[13] Bretherton, *Christ and the Common Life*, 18.
[14] Bretherton, *Christ and the Common Life*, 18.
[15] Bretherton, *Christ and the Common Life*, 18.
[16] Bretherton, *Christ and the Common Life*, 21.
[17] Bretherton, *Christ and the Common Life*, 29-30.
[18] Bretherton, *Christ and the Common Life*, 31. This contrast was first made by Arne Rasmusson in *The Church as Polis: From Political Theology to Theological Politics as Exemplified by Jürgen Moltmann and Stanley Hauerwas* (Notre Dame, IN: University of Notre Dame, 1995).

Politics is not something that is separate from the church, the church is political, as Stanley Hauerwas is fond of saying, 'the church does not have a social ethic; the church is a social ethic.'[19] What I want to attempt in this lecture is to offer an account of a Baptist social ethic, a Baptist politic; what it is within our tradition that forms our political vision and engagement with the world, seeking to acknowledge its strengths and weaknesses. The broader 'ecclesial turn' in political theology[20] requires an acknowledgement and a confession[21] of where our way of being church has not contributed to the flourishing of life.

## The Contribution of Nigel Wright

Wright's Whitley Lecture was a presentation of a Baptist theology of the state. He acknowledges he is not the first Baptist to engage in this area, but he claims that other attempts have been 'surprisingly meagre.'[22] Wright's political theology is centred on an understanding of church and state, captured in the title of his 2005 work: *Free Church, Free State*. Politics begins with the church, it has 'priority of importance' because it is the '*locus* of [God's] mission.'[23] The church, for Wright, is God's 'primary earthly instrument' for the reconciliation

---

[19] Stanley Hauerwas, *The Peaceable Kingdom* (London: SCM, 1983), 99.
[20] The language of 'ecclesial turn' comes from Bretherton, *Christianity and the Contemporary Politics*, 16. It covers the work of Oliver O'Donovan, Stanley Hauerwas, John Milbank, William Cavanaugh and others.
[21] I borrow these two terms from Ryan Andrew Newson, *Inhabiting the World: Identity, Politics and Theology in Radical Baptist Perspective* (Macon, GA: Mercer, 2017), 139.
[22] Wright, *Power and Discipleship*, 12.
[23] Wright, *Power and Discipleship*, 25.

of the world.[24] The church 'stands at variance' to human society shaped by its 'new way of life based upon forgiveness and mutual service.'[25] In this way 'being the Church is a political act.'[26] This distinct way of the church's life reflects its 'missionary nature'[27] as a witnessing community, whose vocation is for the 'whole world.'[28]

The state follows the church in theological ordering, but is nonetheless ordained by God, provisionally, as a current 'means of restraining chaos and anarchy.'[29] Wright sees positive role for the state, although 'one set within certain bounds.'[30] A key word he uses in relation to the state is 'ambivalent' or 'ambiguous.'[31] Behind this, following Walter Wink, is an understanding that the state is one of the powers that is simultaneously good, fallen, and in need of redemption.[32] The state's primary role is 'the maintenance of justice, peace and freedom.'[33] This 'policing' function at its best is 'essential to reducing and overcoming violence.'[34] The state can also have a more beneficial purpose where it is used to 'undergird the weak' and holds a covenantal understanding of humanity that builds and practices community and co-operation. A

---

[24] Wright, *Power and Discipleship*, 26.
[25] Wright, *Power and Discipleship*, 26.
[26] Wright, *Radical Evangelical*, 111.
[27] Wright, *Power and Discipleship*, 26.
[28] Wright, *Power and Discipleship*, 27.
[29] Wright, *Power and Discipleship*, 27.
[30] Wright, *Power and Discipleship*, 27.
[31] Wright, *Power and Discipleship*, 16. Cf. Wright, *Disavowing Constantine*, 184. See also Wright, 'Government as Ambiguous Power.'
[32] Walter Wink, *Unmasking the Powers* (Philadelphia: Fortress, 1986), 67, cited in Wright, *Power and Discipleship*, 17. In the *Radical Kingdom*, 68-69, Wright makes the same point, but draws on Yoder's argument in *The Politics of Jesus*.
[33] Wright, *Power and Discipleship*, 31.
[34] Wright, *Power and Discipleship*, 31.

Baptist political theology supports the state in these aims, but argues clearly that the state should be 'religiously "neutral".'[35] In this way both church and state remain free: neither can impose themselves on the other. This leads him to argue for the disestablishment of the Church of England. 'No consistent Baptist can approve of the sacral state or anything that looks like it.'[36] The state is 'secular', yet should not be 'secularist.'[37] The church and state should not be indifferent; there can, says Wright, be space and opportunity for co-operation, as long as 'religious impartiality' is upheld.

In *Disavowing Constantine*, Wright gives more attention to the relationship between church and state and outlines a position which he later calls 'participating without possessing.'[38] Here I want to focus on two of the theses he presents. First, Wright argues that the cause of Christ can never be advanced by worldly means or alliances with the state.[39] This is an argument for a separation of church from state, what he calls a 'critical distancing.'[40] Wright follows this with the contention that this does not 'imply the separation of church from society' and as such the church 'moulds society wherever possible according to its pattern of social existence in Christ.'[41] This 'moulding' of society' is done by 'faithfully being the church', 'participating constructively in

---

[35] Wright, *Power and Discipleship*, 32.
[36] Wright, *Challenge to Change*, 203, cf. 208-09.
[37] Wright, *Power and Discipleship*, 27-29.
[38] Wright, *Free Church, Free State*, 276. First used in 2003 in a lecture given to the Industrial Christian Fellowship.
[39] Wright, *Disavowing Constantine*, 185.
[40] Wright, *Disavowing Constantine*, 186.
[41] Wright, *Disavowing Constantine*, 187.

the social order and the intermediate structures of society' and through 'political participation.' Faithfully being the church draws on this concept of the church as a witnessing community, a '"pacesetter" for the wider world.'[42] The church has its own politics as 'messianic communities'[43] shaped by the politics of Jesus[44] — which it offers the world. Wright is insistent that any political theology comes from a 'renewed reflection on the meaning of Christ for the complexities of our world.'[45] In *Challenge to Change*, he speaks of a 'positive nonconformity' grounded in Christ-focused living.[46] If he speaks of the ambivalence of the state, he also uses the word 'positive' at various points to articulate a political position that is about what the church is for and not just what it is against.[47] If being faithful says the church stands apart from the world, Wright's other two forms of 'moulding' are about participation in society. This participation is practised not by a gathered church, but a scattered one; Wright switches from the language of the church to that of the Christian:

> individual members of the church will be scattered throughout all organs of society … they will sometimes subvert "the System" when its idolatries become clear; they will sometimes affirm and strength that which corresponds to God's purposes

---

[42] Wright, *Power and Discipleship*, 35.

[43] Wright, *Disavowing Constantine*, 188.

[44] This is of course the title of Yoder's famous book. Wright was reading *The Politics of Jesus* by 1986 when *The Radical Kingdom* was written, and of course Yoder's theology was a key focus of his doctoral work. For some reflections on his relationship to Yoder, see his review of *John Howard Yoder: Radical Theologian* edited by J. Denny Weaver (Eugene, OR: Cascade, 2014) in *Regent's Reviews* 6.2 (April 2015): 25-26. https://www.rpc.ox.ac.uk/wp-content/uploads/2018/05/RR-April-2015.pdf

[45] Wright, *Challenge to Change*, 210.

[46] Wright, *Challenge to Change*, 211.

[47] The subtitle of *Free Church* is 'A Positive Baptist Vision.'

for creation ... they will seek for those modest and sometimes radical improvements which are signs that the world's redemption is near.[48]

This argument for participating without possessing leads Wright to see the possibility of a non-Constantinian Christendom, in which any adherence to the Christian faith, or any faith, is 'gained and maintained through voluntary means alone.'[49] This would have commonality with the historic Baptist position. A Christendom of this kind would be 'the grounding of a healthy, tolerant and free society.'[50] It has similarities with what he terms 'soft secularism.'[51] A hard secularism reduces all religious beliefs and practices to the private sphere, a soft secularism is open to their contribution in the public arena. Wright believes that 'faith groups should have access to public debate and political bodies in recognition of their contribution to the moral formation of citizens, their involvement in local communities and the social capital they generate.'[52] This would be on 'the basis of merit, competence and intellectual coherence.'[53] Wright recognises that his proposed political theology will not be without tension in practice; he says that is 'surely to be expected.'[54] What is necessary is 'to contend for new understandings of what it means to be free.'[55]

---

[48] Wright, *Power and Discipleship*, 35.

[49] Wright, *Free Church*, 276.

[50] Wright, *Free Church*, 277.

[51] Wright, *Free Church*, 277. The term 'soft secularism' Wright borrows from David Fergusson.

[52] Wright, *Free Church*, 278.

[53] Wright, *New Baptists*, 110.

[54] Wright, 'Humane Religion', 30.

[55] Wright, 'Humane Religion', 31. For a critical engagement on Wright and freedom, see John Colwell, 'The Coherence of Freedom: Can Church or State ever be truly free?' in *Challenging to Change: Dialogues with a Radical Baptist Theologian.*

## What shapes a Baptist political theology?

In what follows I want to sketch a Baptist political theology that recognises the church as a political community, to explore further what might be understood when Wright says being the church is a political act and a form of messianic community. What I hope to demonstrate is that the ecclesial convictions of the people called Baptists cannot be anything but political. So where Wright has helped provide an argument for understanding the state, I want to focus more on how we understand the church politically.

As a means of framing my proposal I want to suggest that the Baptist Union of Great Britain's Declaration of Principle[56] can be seen as a containing the main elements of a Baptist political theology. In brief: a focus on the authority of the Lord Jesus Christ, the practices of congregational discernment, believers' baptism, and Christian witness. The Declaration should be understood as political theology. This follows the argument of Paul Fiddes, Brian Haymes, Richard Kidd and Michael Quicke[57] found in *Something to Declare: A Study of the Declaration of Principle* where they claim that the Declaration is 'notably theological' and is 'much more than a statement of

---

*Essays Presented to Dr. Nigel G. Wright on his Sixtieth Birthday* (London: Spurgeon's College, 2009), 39-53.

[56] It was first formulated in 1873, then revised significantly in 1904, followed by smaller revisions in 1906 and 1938. In 2023 it will have held English Baptists in Union together for 150 years.

[57] At the time of writing, the four authors were Principals of the English colleges in members with the Baptist Union.

organisational policy pragmatically to achieve certain ends.'[58] It is, say the authors, a 'covenant document.'[59] The title given to their study, *Something to Declare, is* interesting and begs the question, to whom? Might we see the Declaration as public theology, as a political statement of church identity and purpose? Baptists are thus not a sect;[60] instead Baptists are a free church engaged in and for the society it seeks to witness to and serve with a 'vocation to be part of God's kingdom life in the world.'[61]

I have decided to use the Declaration because it is brief, and because it does have something like a normative status among English Baptists. However, before going further, I should declare (!) that my use of the Declaration should not be taken to suggest that I do not share some of the concern that the likes of John Colwell have expressed over its formulation.[62] While the introduction of the Declaration, especially from its 1904 version onwards, was an astonishing creative summary of Baptist convictions, I believe, with Colwell and others, it could do with some revision — it was after all last revised in 1938 — to make it more precise and persuasive as a basis for covenanting together as English Baptists.

---

[58] Richard Kidd (ed.), *Something to Declare: A Study of the Declaration of Principle* (Didcot: Baptist Union, 1996), 24. I will use the shorthand 'the Declaration' from this point on.

[59] Kidd (ed.), *Something to Declare*, 54.

[60] On the question are Baptists a church or a sect, see Paul Fiddes, 'Church and Sect: Cross-Currents in Early Baptist Life' in *Exploring Baptist Origins* edited by Anthony R. Cross and Nicholas J. Wood (Oxford: Regent's Park College, 2010), 33-57.

[61] Brian Haymes, *A Question of Identity: Reflections on Baptist Identity and Practice* (Leeds: Yorkshire Baptist Association, 1986), 24.

[62] See John Colwell, 'Catholicity and Confessionalism' in *Truth That Never Dies* edited by Nigel Wright (Eugene, OR: Pickwick, 2014), 143-45.

## 1. The Power of the Lord Jesus Christ

The Declaration of Principle begins by stating that 'our Lord and Saviour Jesus Christ, God manifest in the flesh, is the sole and absolute authority in all matters relating to faith and practice.' A Baptist political theology is centred on Jesus, who is addressed as Lord, Saviour, Christ, and God. Baptists work with a 'Christocentric framework.'[63] The 1904 version of the Declaration spoke only of 'our Lord Jesus Christ'; in 1906, to this was added the words, 'our God and Saviour'; and then in 1938 it was revised again, introducing the phrase 'God manifest in the flesh' and this has remained its wording since.[64] Each revision has defined more of who Jesus is and pointing to his incarnation, his life, death, resurrection and ascension. The reference to 'our' at the beginning acknowledges that Jesus cannot be separated from being his disciple, to confess and know Christ as Lord, Saviour and God incarnate is to follow Christ. The 1998 Baptist Union report *5 Core Values for a Gospel People* saw that each perceived core value — prophetic, inclusive, sacrificial, missionary and worshipping — was about 'following Jesus.' The values, it argued, 'flow from and reflect the nature of God as revealed in Jesus Christ.'[65] This focus on Christ is not just in the witness of the four gospels to the life of Jesus or to the Christology of the rest of the New Testament, but to the Jesus who *is*

---

[63] Ian Randall, 'Tracing Baptist Theological Footprints: A European Perspective', *Perspectives in Religious Studies* 36.2 (Summer 2009): 137.
[64] It should be noted that only the first article of the Declaration has been changed since 1904.
[65] *5 Core Values for a Gospel People* (Didcot: Baptist Union, 1999), 3.

Lord, risen and reigning now.[66] A Baptist conviction is that the ascended Jesus is present to the church now.[67]

To name Jesus Lord, Saviour, and God incarnate, is to acknowledge his sole and absolute authority. To speak of authority is to use political language. The claim being made is that power to rule or govern belongs to Christ and to Christ alone. This conviction can be traced back to the earliest Baptists. Thomas Helwys wrote in 1612, 'Christ is King alone, only high priest and chief bishop; and there is no king, no primate, metropolitan, archbishop, lord spiritual, but Christ only, nor may be, either in name or power to exercise authority one over another.'[68] William Kiffin in 1641 likewise claimed that 'Christ is King of his church; and that Christ hath given this power to his church, not to a hierarchy, neither to a national presbytery, but to a company of saints in a congregational way.'[69] Ian Birch states that 'the controlling dynamic of Baptist ecclesiology in the 1640s and 1650s was the expressed intention to organize a church according to the rule of Christ, Priest, Prophet, and King.'[70] A Baptist political theology is centred upon the 'politics of Jesus.'

---

[66] As James McClendon puts it: 'Our question is not past but present: *Is* the risen One who confronts us here and now, today, in the common life of the church — *is* this one true God, true man, one risen Jesus Christ?', *Systematic Theology Vol II: Doctrine* (Nashville: Abingdon, 1994), 239. The answer for McClendon to this question is of course yes.

[67] For an exploration of this theme see Christopher J. Holmes, *Ethics in the Presence of Christ* (London: T & T Clark, 2012).

[68] Thomas Helwys, *A Short Declaration of the Mystery of Iniquity* edited and introduced by Richard Groves (Macon, GA: Mercer, 1998), 34.

[69] Kiffen cited in Curtis Freeman, *Undomesticated Dissent: Democracy and the Public Virtue of Religious Nonconformity* (Waco, TX: Baylor, 2017), 42.

[70] Ian Birch, *To Follow the Lambe Wheresoever He Goeth* (Eugene, OR: Pickwick, 2017), 65.

What is the authority of Jesus like? It is not the authority of the Gentile rulers (Mark 10.42-43). When Jesus says, 'all authority in heaven and earth has been given to me' (Matt. 28.18), we cannot separate his authority from his identity.[71] Earlier in Matthew's gospel Jesus is identified as the servant described by Isaiah 42.1-4 (Matt. 12.17-21). The identity and manner of Jesus who is given all authority challenges other kinds of authority: 'It is the crucified Jesus who reigns'[72] and in being the crucified one is his 'disavowal of the kingship of this world.'[73] Stephen Holmes has recently argued that the key to Baptist identity (still) is 'a belief in the active, direct, Lordship of Christ over every person and over every local congregation.'[74] By direct he means that there are no intermediaries outside of Jesus. By active he means this Lordship is dynamic, addressing believer and church in its present context. The Lord Jesus is where we start from: we look to Jesus (Heb. 12.2).[75]

The scope of Christ's authority is qualified in the Declaration to cover 'matters relating to faith and practice.' This might suggest that there are areas in which Christ does not have sole and absolute authority. For

---

[71] Stanley Hauerwas, *A Community of Character* (Notre Dame, IN: University of Notre Dame, 1981), 45 citing Julian Hartt, *A Christian Critique of America* (Harper and Row, 1967), 166-67.

[72] John Colwell, *Living the Christian Story: The Distinctiveness of Christian Ethics* (Edinburgh: T & T Clark, 2001), 246.

[73] Stanley Hauerwas, *After Christendom* (Nashville: Abingdon, 1991), 91 cited in Colwell, *Living the Christian Story*, 245n.37.

[74] Stephen R. Holmes, 'Baptist Identity, Once More', *Journal of Baptist Theology in Context* 3 (2021): 20-21.

[75] I note here that I am aware that some will be uncomfortable with the language of 'King' and 'Lord.' I use it because the New Testament does, but with the recognition of how Scripture summons us to understand these terms that challenge their usage in other contexts.

example, Helwys recognised the sovereignty of the monarch alongside the sovereignty of Christ. He could write that 'if [Christ] were upon earth in the flesh, he would be subject to our lord the king in his earthly kingdom.'[76] What Helwys sought to argue was the limitation of the monarch's sovereignty, so that in terms of person's religion to God, he famously wrote:

> 'the king shall not answer for it. Neither may the king be judge between God and man. Let them be heretics, Turks, Jews, or whatsoever, it appertains not to the earthly power to punish them in the least measure.'[77]

Otherwise he was content that the king reigned as one ordained by God, although in saying that, Helwys was arguing the king was subject to God.

At the same time, it might be argued that there are no matters unrelated to faith and practice, that it is 'not possible to separate the religious from the social'[78] and any attempt to make faith and practice private should be resisted, that is, the confession Jesus is Lord is a 'determinative political claim.'[79] If Jesus is Lord, he is Lord of all things (Phil 2.8-9). A Baptist political theology, especially one with a tradition of dissent, will live with the tension between the authority of the state and the authority of Christ. The conviction that Baptists have argued for is that the authority of the state is not synonymous with the authority of Christ, and that ultimately, as Holmes argues, is 'a conviction . . . whether acted

---

[76] Helwys, *A Short Declaration*, 34.

[77] Helwys, *A Short Declaration*, 53.

[78] Samuel Wells, 'The Difference Christ Makes' in *The Difference Christ Makes* edited by Charlier Collier (Eugene, OR: Cascade, 2015), 15.

[79] Stanley Hauerwas, *Approaching the End* (Grand Rapids, MI: Eerdmans, 2013), 82.

on or not: religious faithfulness is more important than national identity.'[80]

A Baptist political theology begins with the authority of the Lord Jesus Christ: the baptised believer and the church live 'under the rule of Christ.' The Declaration uses the language of 'law' as reference to the rule of Christ. What is meant by 'His Laws' is not entirely clear. John Colwell thinks it 'reinforces naïve notions of Scripture as a book of rules.'[81] While the authors of *Something to Declare* think that what is being referenced by this phrase is 'the teaching of Christ in the gospels', but suggest that we understand it as 'His purposes and demands on our lives.'[82] Nigel Wright offers the most helpful reading when he says that alongside the teachings of Christ in the New Testament, 'His laws' is also the 'laws, or guidance, he continues to give through the Holy Spirit to the congregations which submit to his rule.'[83] The language of authority and laws points to the church as *polis* with its particular governance and rules provided by Christ, ways known and to be made known.

Knowing what the rule of Christ is, the Declaration states, happens as a congregation reads the Bible under the guidance of the Holy Spirit. This suggests that the politics of Jesus is not obvious, but requires revelation, guidance and interpretation. The Holy Scriptures have authority

---

[80] Holmes, 'Our Story Begins in Exile', 29 April 2016. http://steverholmes.org.uk/blog/?p=7611.
[81] Colwell, 'Catholicity and Confessionalism', 144.
[82] Kidd (ed.), *Something to Declare*, 33.
[83] Nigel Wright, 'Spirituality as Discipleship: the Anabaptist Heritage' in *Under the Rule of Christ* edited by Paul S. Fiddes (Macon, GA: Smyth & Helwys, 2008), 87.

because they witness to the authority of Christ, they lead us to the confession that Jesus is Lord, Saviour, Christ and God manifest in the flesh. Christ, Scripture and Holy Spirit are bound in relationship with a listening congregation. A Baptist hermeneutic will be christologically-shaped and penumatologically-inspired. This emphasis on the direct, active Lordship of Christ through Scripture and the leading of the Holy Spirit means a Baptist political theology will always in a sense be provisional; its practices and politics will always be open to the word of Christ to the congregation. Steven Harmon characterizes this as

> Baptist churches at their best are relentlessly pilgrim communities that resist all overly realized eschatologies of the church. Their ecclesial ideal is the church that is fully under the rule of Christ, which they locate somewhere ahead of them rather than in any past or present instantiation of the church.[84]

## 2. The Politics of the Church Meeting

The Declaration says that 'each Church has liberty … to interpret and administer His laws.' Where does this happen? It happens in a myriad of places, but for Baptists, centrally it has taken place in the practice of the Church Meeting.

Alongside believers' baptism (which we will address next), the other key distinctive church practice among Baptists is that of the Church Meeting, which Holmes describes as 'a profoundly subversive and

---

[84] Steven R. Harmon, *Baptist Identity and the Ecumenical Future* (Waco, TX: Baylor, 2016), 224-25.

political act.'[85] The Church Meeting is a politics in action. A Baptist political theology is profoundly local in practice (and to this we will return later). It was from its beginnings counter-cultural. Long before all citizens in the UK were given the vote, Baptists gave all members, women and men,[86] rich or poor, a vote, demonstrating a conviction that all were equal before God and all were competent in the act of discernment.[87] It might be said that the Church Meeting is simply an example of democracy, but this would not be the way Baptists have understood what is taking place. As Paul Fiddes says, 'the church meeting is not "people power" in the sense of simply counting votes and canvassing a majority … the aim [instead] is to search for consent about the mind of Christ.'[88] Elsewhere Fiddes refers to the practice in the seventeenth century where the Church Meeting would follow the Lord's Supper. The record of the church minutes was kept in a draw below the communion Table, symbolising, suggests Fiddes, 'the sacramental significance' of both the Supper and the Meeting.[89] The congregation acknowledges that Christ is the sole and absolute authority, and the Church Meeting gathers to discern Christ's will. The

---

[85] Stephen Holmes, 'Knowing Together the Mind of Christ: Congregational Government and the Church Meeting' in *Questions of Identity: Studies in Honour of Brian Haymes* edited by Anthony R. Cross and Ruth Gouldbourne (Oxford: Regent's Park College, 2011), 175.

[86] See Ruth Gouldbourne, *Reinventing the Wheel: Women and Ministry in Baptist Life* (Oxford: Whitley, 1997), 9-10.

[87] Holmes, 'Knowing Together the Mind of Christ', 181.

[88] Paul S. Fiddes, *Tracks and Traces: Baptist Identity in Church and Theology* (Carlisle: Paternoster, 2003), 86.

[89] Paul S. Fiddes, *Participating in God* (London: DLT, 2000), 283. Colwell also speaks of 'a promised sacramental dynamic' based on the promised presence of Jesus in Matt 18.20, 'Integrity and Relatedness', *Baptist Quarterly* 48.1 (2017): 19.

key characteristic of the Baptist Church Meeting is the practice of discernment: the members of the church gathering together to seek the mind of Christ for its life, worship, and mission. This discernment takes the form of listening — of listening to Scripture, to the guidance of the Holy Spirit, to views of the members, and to views or resources from beyond the congregation[90] — that a consensus might be found to what Christ is saying. This is a communal hermeneutics, where the congregation is 'always on the way and in the fray.'[91] 'Always on the way' meaning that the act of discernment never finishes, the church's knowledge of the mind of Christ is always incomplete; and 'in the fray' pointing out that the church meeting can be a place of disagreement or where the way forward is unclear. Alongside the practice of the Church Meeting are therefore needed practices of friendship and worship which enable the church to find reconciliation and resolution,[92] in the face of tension and dispute.

---

[90] Views might come from wider ecclesial bodies, in England, this might be the Council or the Assembly of the Baptist Union, or from an Association or local network of churches. See *The Nature of the Assembly and the Council of Great Britain* (Didcot: Baptist Union, 1994) for one account to offer a theology. For possible resources from beyond the local congregation see Amy L. Chilton and Steven R. Harmon (eds.), *Sources of Light: Resources for Baptist Churches Practicing Theology* (Macon GA: Mercer, 2020), who suggest twenty-three different resources from contextual theologies, confessions of faith, liturgies, and ecumenism.

[91] This phrase is the title of Helen Dare's 2014 Whitley Lecture. Another way of describing this would be to say that the authority of the church meeting is 'proximate', see McClendon, *Doctrine*, 480.

[92] On friendship see Sean F. Winter, 'Persuading Friends: Friendship and Testimony in Baptist Interpretative Communities' in *The 'Plainly Revealed' Word of God: Baptist Hermeneutics in Theory and Practice* edited by Helen Dare and Simon Woodman (Macon, GA: Mercer, 2011), 253-70. On worship, and in particular the Lord's Supper, see Helen Dare, 'Remembering our Hermeneutics: Baptists Reconciling (with) Interpretative Diversity' in *Reconciling Rites: Essays in Honour*

Within the church and the Church Meeting 'oversight flows to and fro between the personal and the communal'[93] — it does not reside solely with the ministers, or the deacons, or the members, but is instead 'dynamic', with any decisions made a product of trust, patience, and humility.[94] Leadership is shared and meetings are multi-voiced.[95] Ruth Moriarty has recently coined the phrase 'slow wisdom' to describe the practice of the Church Meeting done well.[96] This is a politics that takes time, that is not frenetic, that refuses to rush. It embodies Bretherton's prescriptions for democratic politics: people before program, politics before procedure, and practice before theory.[97] One of the reasons for a slow politics is that while different members can bring their varying knowledge and experience in practical matters like finance, fabric, health and safety, etc. — indicating there is a place for expertise — at the same time, Holmes argues that 'in the matter of discerning the mind of Christ, everyone present is always utterly incompetent, unless and until Christ should graciously aid them by the Spirit.'[98]

---

*of Myra N. Blyth* edited by Andy Goodliff, Anthony Clarke and Beth Allison-Glenny (Oxford: Regent's Park College, 2020), 48-70.

[93] Fiddes, *Tracks and Traces*, 87.

[94] On trust see Richard Kidd (ed.), *On the Way of Trust* (Oxford: Whitley, 1997). On patience see David Bunce, 'The Theological Virtue of Patience in Church Life', a paper given at Theology Live 2019 and also Andrew Ryan Newson, *Radical Friendship: The Politics of Communal Discernment* (Philadelphia: Fortress, 2017), 146-51. On humility see Samuel Wells, *Walk Humbly* (Norwich: Canterbury, 2019) and Newson, *Radical Friendship*, 60-64.

[95] See Ruth Gouldbourne, 'Voices', *Baptist Ministers' Journal* 268 (October 1999), 6-9.

[96] See Ruth Moriarty, 'Slow Wisdom and the Baptist practice of discernment', a paper given at Theology Live 2020. She also her forthcoming doctoral thesis from the University of Chester: 'How Do Baptists Discern the Mind of Christ?'

[97] Bretherton, *Christ and the Common Life*, 453-60.

[98] Holmes, 'Knowing Together the Mind of Christ', 184.

The Church Meeting is under the authority of Christ and seeks the guidance of the Holy Spirit, yet it is also a meeting of human beings each of whom is an 'unsatisfactory Christian.'[99] The Church Meeting can be, and no doubt has been and is, an arena for sexism, racism, classism, and other prejudices. Rather than listening, Church Meetings can be a place of silencing and exclusion of voices. The politics of the Church Meeting does not always match the vision that we have for it. For this reason Colwell can speak of the need for the 'renewal'[100] of the Church Meeting, echoed years earlier by Wright, who wrote of 'redeeming' the Church Meeting from its 'distortions.'[101] Here one of the weaknesses of a Baptist politics, which can contribute to the Church Meeting as a distorting practice[102] is the localism of the congregation, to which we now turn.

'*Each* Church has liberty' says the Declaration, meaning that a Baptist political theology will first be local. At the same time the affirmation of the Declaration, by ministers and churches, is also to belong to the Baptist Union, and in nearly all cases, this will mean in addition belonging to a regional Association (before 2002 Associations were generally smaller and organised around county boundaries).[103] A

---

[99] See Stanley Hauerwas, *The Work of Theology* (Grand Rapids, MI: Eerdmans, 2015), 267. The term was used initially by Nicholas Healy in *Hauerwas: A (Very) Critical Introduction* (Grands Rapids, MI: Eerdmans, 2014).

[100] Colwell, 'Integrity and Relatedness', 18.

[101] Nigel Wright, *Challenge to Change* (Eastbourne: Kingsway, 1991), 91-132.

[102] Newson, drawing on McClendon, sees that practices can be 'powerfully life-giving and powerfully destructive' including those that constitute church, *Inhabiting the World*, 140.

[103] For a history of the changes see Andy Goodliff, *Renewing a Modern Denomination* (Eugene: OR: Pickwick, 2020).

Baptist political theology will first be local, but it will also recognise a wider form of ecclesial community as well, although how 'ecclesial' has varied.[104] An emphasis on the local means that nearly all Baptists will always be sensitive and suspicious to anything that is, or even feels like, centralisation. A reading of Baptist works through the twentieth century show the tension between those for whom the local is supreme and those who believed the local must always be balanced with a real sense of catholicity.[105] There is a strength to this localism of a church. It brings a greater sense of participation and involvement in the life, mission and discernment of a congregation.[106] There is an intensity of relationship, built on a history of friendship walking together in prayer and action. Decisions are made by the people under Christ and not imposed from outside. At its best, the local church generates a politics that is attentive to people and place in and beyond the church members.[107] A local church is an 'acted creed':[108] 'this is what we believe Christ is saying to us here in this place at this time.'

---

[104] Some have argued that Association and Union should be understood as a strategic alliance or a resource agency, others have argued for these bodies as ecclesial in nature, as expressions of 'being church'.

[105] Compare Alec Gilmore (ed.), *The Pattern of the Church* (Lutterworth, 1962) with *Liberty in the Lord* (London: Baptist Revival Fellowship, 1964).

[106] See Wright, 'Spirituality as Discipleship', 85-88 and Wright, *New Baptists, New Agenda*, 64-80.

[107] One of my favourite essays of Stanley Hauerwas is where he describes where he goes to church, at the time Aldersgate United Methodist Church, see 'In Defense of Cultural Christianity' in *Sanctify Them in the Truth* (Edinburgh: T & T Clark, 1998), 157-73.

[108] The language of 'acted creed' first appears (as far as is known) in an article by Henry Wheeler Robinson in 1904 in reference to baptism (Anthony R. Cross, *Baptism and the Baptists* [Carlisle: Paternoster, 2000], 31), and appears also in the 1948 Baptist Union statement 'The Baptist Doctrine of the Church.' I'm using it here in an ecclesial sense.

At the same time a focus on the local can create a congregation that is suffocating, heretical and destructive. Those who advocate for the independence of the church are sometimes not far from a kind of idolatry. Here, as others have observed, the Declaration speaks of the liberty of the church not its independence.[109] From as early as the 1640s, Baptist congregations were associating together. As the 1644 London Confession states:

> And although the particular Congregations be distinct and severall Bodies, every one a compact and knit Citie in it selfe; yet are they all to walk by one and the same Rule, and by all meanes convenient to have the counsell and help of another in all needful affaires of the Church, as members of one body in the common faith under Christ their onely head.[110]

A congregation, in the words of P. T. Forsyth, is an 'outcrop' of the total and continuous church.[111] John Insore Essick and Mark Medley have argued that Baptists need to acknowledge what they call a 'local catholicity' where 'both mutually inform one another.'[112] Attention to catholicity — to other peoples and places 'who walk by one and the same Rule' — calls the local congregation to see that while it is fully a church, it is not the whole church. The local church in fellowship with other churches enables its flourishing, and when welcomed as a means of the guidance of the Holy Spirit, can protect or correct the church from the demonic.

---

[109] Kidd (ed.), *Something to Declare*, 33.

[110] Lumpkin (ed.), *Baptist Confessions of Faith* (Valley Forge: Judson, 1969), 168-69.

[111] P. T. Forsyth, *The Church and the Sacraments* (1917) cited in Ernest Payne, *The Fellowship of the Believers* (London: Carey Kingsgate, 1952), 29n.6.

[112] Mark Medley and John Insore Essick, 'Local catholicity: The bodies and places where Jesus is (found)', *Review and Expositor* 112.1 (2015), 55.

## 3. The Politics of Baptism

The second article of the Declaration of Principle is on baptism: 'That Christian Baptism is the immersion in water into the Name of the Father, the Son, and the Holy Ghost, of those who have professed repentance towards God and faith in our Lord Jesus Christ.' A Baptist political theology will recognise the practice of believers' baptism as political. At the time that the Baptist story in England began all children were expected to be baptised 'on the basis they belonged to the national church.'[113] To refrain from doing so was clearly a political act.

Philip Thompson has argued that the Baptist practice of believers' baptism 'set the boundary that situated and gave proper significance to all human bodies: individual, communal or political.'[114] Thompson reads the Baptist practice of baptism in light of Peter Berger's argument in *The Sacred Canopy*.[115] Berger understands that meaning in a society is enabled by 'processes of legitimation' of which 'religion has been the most effective and widely used ... throughout human history.'[116] Thompson argues that this legitimating function was performed by the English Church and State, especially in the 1662 Act of Uniformity and

---

[113] Birch, *To Follow the Lambe*, 39. See also, Stephen Wright, *Early English Baptists* (Woodbridge: Boydell, 2006), 1.

[114] Philip E. Thompson, 'Sacraments and Religious Liberty: From Critical Practice to Rejected Infringement' in *Baptist Sacramentalism* edited by Anthony R. Cross and Philip E. Thompson (Carlisle: Paternoster, 2003), 46. He's drawing on the phrasing of Graham Ward in 'Bodies: The Displaced Body of Jesus Christ' in *Radical Orthodoxy* edited by John Milbank, Catherine Pickstock and Graham Ward (London: Routledge, 1999), 176.

[115] Peter L . Berger, *The Sacred Canopy: Elements of a Sociological Theory of Religion* (New York: Doubleday, 1967).

[116] Thompson, 'Sacraments and Religious Liberty', 41.

the 1673 Test Act. This was used against Baptists and other dissenters to bar them from full citizenship. The Baptist response was to see this view of society as a 'false god ... built upon idolatry.'[117] The conviction of the Baptists, says Thompson, was the freedom of God, which they saw being 'usurped' by the requirements in law.[118]

For the early Baptists then, baptism had political dimensions: 'it relativized all other political expressions by locating the true politics within the church.'[119] Thompson understands the baptised believers' community as 'the interruption and delegitimization of the idolatrous politics of the state.'[120] Barry Harvey writes that 'the sacraments [meaning baptism and Eucharist] in particular propel the members of Christ's body beyond the boundaries in which state and market seek to confine us by binding us together in a new political association.'[121] In being baptised, the believer acknowledged that 'true government lay ... in the politics of the risen and ascended Lord.'[122] To undergo baptism as a believer and to refrain from practising infant baptism was a form of dissent from the norms of established church and the state. It recognised the claim of Christ on the believer to be more determinative than other claims, including those of national citizenship. Baptism is into Christ and his body (the church) and not into the nation-state.

---

[117] Thompson, 'Sacraments and Religious Liberty', 45.

[118] Thompson, 'Sacraments and Religious Liberty', 44. See Philip E. Thompson, 'People of the Free God: The Passion of Seventeenth Century Baptists', *American Baptist Quarterly* 15.3 (September 1996): 233-41.

[119] Thompson, 'Sacraments and Religious Liberty', 46.

[120] Thompson, 'Sacraments and Religious Liberty', 46.

[121] Barry Harvey, *Baptists and the Catholic Tradition* (Grand Rapids, MI: Baker, 2020), 133.

[122] Thompson, 'Sacraments and Religious Liberty', 46.

Baptism creates the church as a distinct community within a nation and society.

Baptists have not given much attention to the politics of baptism; this reflects a wider issue that Baptists have been more interested in the mode and form of baptism than it's meaning.[123] In one place though Brian Haymes has argued for baptism as a political act: 'baptism is political, carrying considerable ethical significance, raising as it does basic questions of identity, allegiance, and obedience.'[124] Haymes roots his argument in what the New Testament says about Christ and the Powers, drawing on the work of Hendrikus Berkhof and John Howard Yoder.[125] Where the apostle Paul speaks of the 'principalities and the powers' the contention, according to Haymes, is that he understands these as 'structures or systems of earthly existence.'[126] Our experience of the Powers is both positive and negative, in their negative form they are 'oppressive, even tyrannical.' Baptism into Christ is both a dying and rising,[127] where 'the Powers exposed for what they are and where new possibilities for liberated living emerge.'[128] The Declaration says baptism is the immersion into the Name of the Trinity who in the person

---

[123] Christopher J. Ellis, *Gathering: A Theology and Spirituality of Worship in Free Church Tradition* (London: SCM, 2004), 201.

[124] Haymes, 'Baptism as a Political Act' in *Reflections on the Water* edited by Paul S. Fiddes (Macon, GA: Smyth & Helwys, 1996), 77.

[125] Hendrikus Berkhof, *Christ and the Powers* (Waterloo, Ont: Herald, 1962); John Howard Yoder, *The Politics of Jesus* (Grand Rapids, MI: Eerdmans, 1972).

[126] Haymes, 'Baptism as a Political Act', 71.

[127] Romans 6 being the key baptismal text for Baptists. Ruth Gouldbourne says 'Baptists have normatively taken Romans 6.3-14 as central to our understanding of baptism', 'Story-Telling, Sacraments and Sexuality' in *Questions of Identity* (Oxford: Regent's Park College, 2011), 240n.2.

[128] Haymes, 'Baptism as a Political Act', 77.

of the Son 'died ... was buried, and rose again.' In baptism we come to indwell the gospel story: 'we are buried with him and raised with him; ... his story becomes our story.'[129] The newly baptised Christian pledges to follow Christ alongside those who have also been baptised and in serving the Lord 'the church will be ... an alternative society.'[130] Baptism creates a "new mode of social relations within the community';[131] relations of class are replaced by relations of fellowship.[132] The implications of this are that the baptised community go on naming and confronting the powers — political, economic — and live with 'all the political consequences' of confessing Christ is Lord.[133] Following Thompson and Haymes, and their interpretations of early Baptist history and the New Testament, Baptists should see that a political theology is present in the practice of baptism and this is strongly evident in their practice of believers' baptism where the candidate declares their allegiance to Christ, and so also their turning from sin and their rejection of evil. Believers' baptism is a 'disciples' baptism', that is, 'it is a moment for taking up the responsibilities of carrying our cross, suffering opposition for the sake of Christ, and sharing in the mission of God in the world.'[134] Baptism in the early church was political; the early Baptists were part of a recovery of this dimension; the issue today is for Baptists to live again with a 'baptised

---

[129] John Colwell, *Promise and Presence* (Milton Keynes: Paternoster, 2005), 121.
[130] Haymes, 'Baptism as a Political Act', 78.
[131] Harvey, *Baptists and the Catholic Tradition*, 189.
[132] Bretherton, *Christ and the Common Life*, 219.
[133] Haymes, 'Baptism as a Political Act', 82. For a similar argument see Newson, *Inhabiting the World*, 72-75.
[134] Fiddes, *Tracks and Traces*, 136.

imagination', where baptism becomes a political 'liturgy for life.'[135] Baptism becomes not something that happened once in our past, but is a remembering sign: 'remember your baptism' is the word of the preacher.[136]

If baptism is understood as a confrontation of the Powers, it can equally become a Power itself. Ryan Andrew Newson writes of how the baptism of African slaves was a 'tool not of conversion but coercion' in which baptism was 'readily coopted to support the system of white supremacy.'[137] Ruth Gouldbourne shows how the practice of believers' baptism has been (and perhaps still is) gendered. On the one hand it challenged gender for 'no distinction was made between the male and female believer in the practice of baptism.' And yet, it remained gendered in how those being baptised dressed — 'women's [bodies] were shrouded and hampered', so that 'even in that moment there were a series of assumptions about being female and being baptised that came from and looped back to shape assumptions about women, church and God.'[138] The refusal or reluctance to baptise people with learning difficulties demonstrates an understanding of baptism that over-emphasises the verbal articulation of faith.[139] In these and other ways,

---

[135] See Kevin J. Adams, *Living Under the Water* (Grand Rapids, MI: Eerdmans, 2022).
[136] The language of 'remembering sign' comes from James McClendon, *Doctrine*, 386. For one example from a Baptist preacher, see Rodney Wallace Kennedy, 'Remember Your Baptism' in *Sermons from Mind and Heart* (Eugene, OR: Wipf & Stock, 2011), 98-102.
[137] Newson, *Inhabiting the World*, 136. He draws on Katie M. Grimes, 'Breaking the Body of Christ', *Political Theology* 18.1 (January 2017): 22-43.
[138] Gouldbourne, 'Story-telling, Sacraments and Sexuality', 244.
[139] For one response see Sally Nelson, 'A Reflection on Baptism', *Baptist Ministers' Journal* 340 (October 2018): 28-29.

the practice of baptism can go against the politics of baptism in which there is 'no Jew or Greek, slave or free, male and female' (Gal. 3.28).

## 4. The Politics of Mission

The final article of the Declaration of Principle says 'that it is the duty of every disciple to bear witness to the Gospel of Jesus Christ and to take part in the evangelization of the world.' Every disciple is enlisted into God's missionary purposes. It must be noted here that some find the language of 'duty' here unhelpful. Colwell says 'we are constrained by love before we are constrained by obligation.'[140] And the College Principals in *Something to Declare* see duty as overemphasising 'unaided choosing' over a sense instead of participating, through baptism, in the life and mission of God.[141] A minor revision would be to change the line to: 'it is the duty and joy of every disciple', borrowing the language of the Church of England's Eucharistic prayer.[142] Putting the wording to one side, what this third article demonstrates is that 'bearing witness to the Gospel of Jesus Christ' is a 'constitutive part of our identity,'[143] it is part of what it is to be Baptist. Colwell here would argue that it cannot be anything but part of our identity because 'the Church's mission is constituted simply and solely by its being sent into the world.'[144]

What is the Gospel of Jesus Christ? To read the second article of the Declaration, it must be said the Gospel is that 'Jesus died for our sins

---

[140] Colwell, 'Catholicity and Confessionalism', 145.

[141] Kidd (ed.), *Something to Declare*, 48.

[142] Colwell makes a gesture in this direction in 'Integrity and Relatedness', 16.

[143] Nigel Wright, *New Baptists, New Agenda* (Carlisle: Paternoster, 2002), 94.

[144] John Colwell, 'Mission as Ontology', *Baptist Ministers' Journal* 295 (2006): 9.

according to the Scriptures; was buried, and rose again the third day.' I would suggest, following others,[145] that the gospel is helpfully understood by the word 'apocalyptic' in that the Gospel declares that in the life, death and resurrection of Jesus the old has gone and the new has come (2 Cor 5.17). An apocalyptic gospel will always be a political gospel because it makes the claim the world has been rectified in Jesus who is Lord.[146] To bear witness to this gospel will always be a political act because 'the story of Jesus is the story of a new creation, the telling of which cannot but challenge the reigning stories that legitimate the practices of the old age.'[147] It is, in the words of Acts to 'turn the world upside down' and this is not something always welcomed.[148] Mission — evangelism — is political.

For a Baptist political theology it is important that the three articles of the Declaration are read together and not individually. What ties the three articles into one is the Great Commission at the end of Matthew's gospel, where Jesus says, 'All authority ... has been given to me. Therefore go and make disciples of all nations, baptising them in the name of the Father and of the Son and of the Holy Spirit, and teaching them to obey everything I have commanded you.' This is the obvious

---

[145] I reference here just two books for the sake of brevity: *Apocalyptic and the Future of Theology* edited by Joshua B. Davis and Douglas Harink (Eugene, OR: Cascade, 2012) and Philip G. Ziegler, *Militant Grace: The Apocalyptic Turn and the Future of Christian Theology* (Grand Rapids, MI: Baker, 2018).

[146] For a Pauline version of this, see Douglas Campbell, 'Paul's Apocalyptic Politics', *Pro Ecclesia* 22.2 (2013).

[147] Stanley Hauerwas, *Approaching the End* (Grand Rapids, MI: Eerdmans), 45.

[148] For a fascinating (political and apocalyptic) reading of the book of Acts, see C. Kavin Rowe, *World Upside Down* (Oxford: Oxford University Press, 2009).

inspiration to the structure and content of the Declaration.[149] Here is evidence of what Holmes calls the Baptist 'mimetic' approach to the New Testament: Baptists do what they read.[150] So the dutiful disciple who bears witness cannot be other than one who has been baptised and made a member of a church that lives under the rule of Christ. Mission, says Chris Ellis, is 'placed under the authority of Christ.'[151] General Baptists Thomas Lambe, John Griffith, and Edward Barber in the mid-1640s would preacher regularly on evangelism in 'accordance with the "Royal Commission of King Jesus".'[152]

For Baptists this conviction to 'bear witness' to the Gospel has at different times found that this has meant suffering for political reasons. Richard Kidd argues for suffering as 'a defining experience' for Baptists.[153] Baptists in the seventeenth century suffered for their convictions about the gospel. They believed that in bearing witness they were 'pushing back the AntiChristian darkness that covered England.'[154] They were an apocalyptic people. They expected the return of Christ and believed that their task was to build the New Jerusalem. They interpreted both the Roman Catholic Church and the Church of

---

[149] John Howard Shakespeare, General Secretary of the Union at the beginning of the twentieth century, is reported to have said that the whole Declaration is based on 'the words Christ gave to His Disciples when He left them', Kidd (ed.), *Something to Declare*, 20-21.
[150] Holmes, 'Baptist Identity, Once More', 14.
[151] Ellis, *Gathering*, 234.
[152] Ruth Butterfield, 'The Royal Commission of King Jesus', *Baptist Quarterly* 35.2 (April 1993): 56. These words come from the full title of a publication by Edward Barber, *A True Discovery of the Ministry of the Gospell* (1645).
[153] Richard Kidd, 'Spirituality in Suffering: A Defining Experience' in *Under the Rule of Christ* edited by Paul S. Fiddes (Macon, GA: Smyth and Helwys, 2008), 59-78.
[154] Mark R. Bell, *Apocalypse How? Baptist Movements During the English Revolution* (Macon, GA: Mercer, 2000), 43.

31

England as the two beasts mentioned in Revelation 13. They bore witness, but most would not bear arms.[155]

Kidd refers to Barber, who wrote that 'they are not to flee persecution but to "lay down their lives for the publishing and defence of the Gospel if God called them to it."'[156] Kidd also references the witness of Agnes Beaumont, a member of John Bunyan's Bedford church from 1672, whose 'enthusiastic commitment to a dissenting faith, found herself the object of scurrilous accusations against her character.'[157] In his more extensive study, Raymond Brown titles his work on English Nonconformity between 1660-1689 as *Spirituality in Adversity*.[158] The resources of the dissenters to face this adversity, Brown argues, were a dependence on God, identification with Christ and equipping by the Holy Spirit. Bearing witness was costly.

Kidd also provides examples of similar suffering more recently faced by Baptists in South Africa, El Salvador, and Georgia. While suffering for the gospel is not unique to Baptists, Kidd and Brown demonstrate that 'bearing witness' has political consequences. The inclusion of the word 'to bear' indicates that witness is sometimes that which is

---

[155] The refusal to use military action was because they were not Anabaptists, and in particular the Anabaptists of Munster. In addition, they took seriously the words of Paul in Romans 13, and in their eyes the Beast was a mixed civil and ecclesiastical power, and they did not want to do the same. See Bell, *Apocalypse How?*, 30-31.

[156] Kidd, 'Spirituality in Suffering', 63 quoting Edward Barber, *A True Discovery of the Ministery of the Gospel* (1645), cited in B. R. White, *English Baptists in the Seventeenth Century* (Didcot: Baptist Historical Society, 1996), 31.

[157] Kidd, 'Spirituality in Suffering', 64-65.

[158] Raymond Brown, *Spirituality in Adversity: English Nonconformity in a Period of Repression, 1660-1689* (Milton Keynes: Paternoster, 2012).

endured, as evidenced in the one who is named Lord and Saviour (Heb 12.2).

The emphasis on the 'evangelisation of the world' also indicates that the Gospel of Jesus Christ is universal. It is not constrained by borders or cultures. It is good news for everyone, and for Baptists, there has always been a special emphasis, from Helwys to the present, on the freedom to proclaim and the freedom to respond to the Gospel. However, it cannot be ignored that the way that Christians, including Baptists, have undergone evangelism, has not always been experienced as good news. The church has found itself bearing witness not to the gospel of Jesus Christ, but to a gospel that has been accommodated to a different politics. Brian Stanley offers a telling of the history of Protestant mission, including that of the Baptist Missionary Society, in his book *The Bible and the Flag*, which traces how 'their vision was frequently clouded by national and racial pride' and their understanding of justice 'too easily moulded to fit the contours of prevailing Western ideologies.'[159] In another account of the history of Christianity and colonialism, *The Christian Imagination,* the author (a Baptist) Willie James Jennings, argues that Christianity has 'a diseased social imagination.'[160] The use of the present tense rather than the past tense

---

[159] Brian Stanley, *The Bible and the Flag: Protestant Missions and British Imperialism in the Nineteenth and Twentieth Centuries* (Leicester: Apollos, 1990), 184. See also, Brian Stanley 'Nineteenth-century liberation theology: Nonconformist missionaries and imperialism', *Baptist Quarterly* 32:1 (January 1987): 5-18 and 'Baptists, Antislavery and the Legacy of Imperialism', *Baptist Quarterly* 42.4 (2007): 284-95.

[160] Willie James Jennings, *The Christian Imagination: Theology and the Origins of Race* (New Haven, NY: Yale, 2010), 6.

here is because Jennings contends that Christians continue to operate with this diseased social imagination and so are 'without the ability to discern how its intellectual and pedagogical performances reflect and fuel the problem.'[161] Jennings believes that the response required is a theological one, that begins with the recognition, first, that we are Gentiles, and second, that we are creatures.[162]

If the church lives under the rule of Christ, how it undertakes bearing witness and evangelism must be congruent with that rule. The politics of the church is not just how it organises itself as a community, but how it engages as a community with the world. Paul Fiddes' perspective on mission, shaped by a theology of covenant, argues that it should be 'essentially relational ... open in risky welcome' and as such

> offer prophetic criticism of competitive individualism in society, and seek to encourage political and economic policies that are committed to inter-personal relationships; it will also have a care for the whole natural creation, seeking to foster organic relations between all animal and plant life, in partnership with humanity and beyond it.[163]

He concludes his exploration of mission and liberty by saying

> If mission is done in the spirit of Jesus, this means the mood of the suffering servant. Witness to the world is a sharing in the sacrifice of Christ, a kind of "martyrdom", a participation in God's passion for the world. It is thus illegitimate to speak of "aggressive evangelism" or to use the language of military campaigns to describe mission. Mission can never be imperialistic or competitive. It must not be to impose an alien culture upon people, or make them dependent upon an outside agency. Telling the story of Jesus can only be accompanied by

---

[161] Jennings, *The Christian Imagination*, 6-7.
[162] See also Jennings other works, including a commentary on *Acts* (Louisville, KY: WJK, 2017) and *After Whiteness* (Grand Rapids, MI: Eerdmans, 2020).
[163] Fiddes, *Tracks and Traces*, 253-54.

humble pleading; it should never be characterized by coercion, manipulation, the offering of material inducements or any methods that violate the conscience of persons made in the image of God.[164]

## 5. Politics of Dissent

In his George Beasley-Murray Memorial Lecture, John Colwell criticises the Baptist Union and Church of England report, *Pushing at the Boundaries of Unity*, for making 'no explicit mention of a tradition of dissent as defining of Baptist life,' which he suggests, is 'even more basic in English Baptist history … than is baptism itself.'[165] What is perhaps only implicit in the Declaration of Principle — present perhaps in the language of 'each Church has *liberty*' — but explicit in any account of Baptist life over four centuries is a politics of dissent.

Baptists were dissenters. It is not clear whether this is still the case.[166] Many Christians in the late sixteenth and early seventeenth century were dissenters, but the majority saw their dissent from within the Church of England. These Puritans were advocating for reform of the Church. There were some more radical Puritans, given the name Separatists, who felt the Church of England was beyond reform, and so separated themselves from the Church into their own congregations. For some this separation was permanent and amongst their number were the first Baptists. The result of their separation was that the Baptist

---

[164] Fiddes, *Tracks and Traces*, 272-73.

[165] Colwell, 'Catholicity and Confessionalism', 138.

[166] Arguably, the embrace of the language of 'free church' in the later nineteenth century unwittingly enabled a tradition of dissent to be obscured.

story 'begins in exile.'[167] It was in the Netherlands in Amsterdam, not England, that John Smyth and Thomas Helwys founded the first Baptist congregation as they underwent believers' baptism. The first Baptists were part of a 'tiny minority' whose dissent was radical and 'highly eccentric.'[168]

The history of Baptists has been a history of dissent, what can be called, following Alasdair MacIntyre, 'a tradition of dissent.'[169] Curtis Freeman's recent study of John Bunyan, Daniel Defoe and William Blake in *Undomesticated Dissent* is an attempt to recover dissent as a tradition. Crucial to Freeman's argument is that dissent is not just a no to something, but is, more importantly, 'grounded in a profound "Yes!",' which he defines as a yes 'to Jesus Christ as Lord, to God alone as sovereign over conscience, and to the gathered community where Jesus Christ reigns and is discerned together.'[170]

The relationship of monarchy, state and Church in England, meant that any dissent from the Church was political. Freeman notes that the 'beliefs and practices [of Dissenters] were regarded as the seeds of both religious chaos and social anarchy.'[171] Dissenters were the subjects of persecution, fines and imprisonment. While maintaining their

---

[167] Holmes, 'Our Story Begins in Exile.'

[168] John Coffey, 'Church and State, 1550-1750' in *The T & T Clark Companion to Nonconformity* edited by Robert Pope (London: T & T Clark, 2016), 51-52.

[169] See Freeman, *Undomesticated Dissent*, 13-14 drawing on Alasdair MacIntyre, *After Virtue* (Notre Dame IN: University of Notre Dame, 1981) and *Three Rival Versions of Moral Enquiry* (Notre Dame, IN: University of Notre Dame, 1990). Cf. Steven Harmon, *Towards Baptist Catholicity* (Milton Keynes: Paternoster, 2006), 66-69.

[170] Freeman, *Undomesticated Dissent*, 5.

[171] Freeman, *Undomesticated Dissent*, 26.

convictions around conscience and the liberty of the church, Baptists contended strongly that they were good citizens. To be Baptist was not to be *against* the nation, rather it was to be *for* the nation, but without being coerced in faith and practice. This was the place in which Baptists (and other dissenters) struggled to be heard. A Baptist political theology is not one of separation, instead, as Colwell states,

> Dissenters (like Catholics) traditionally have shown little reluctance in seeking involvement and influence in government: the well-being of society is too important to be abandoned to the forces of secularism (or Anglicanism); the claims of Christ demand rather than deny involvement. The tradition of Dissent, then, far from advocating a religion-less State (as if such an entity were possible or conceivable), actively sought to influence the State religiously and resisted (for the most part passively) the marginalisation of its witness.[172]

The practices of church meeting, baptism and witness undergirded by the rule of Christ as king that we have explored should produce a Baptist political theology engaged with the state and society.

Mark Bell in his excellent study of Baptists in the seventeenth century, *Apocalypse How?*, sees a tension among Baptists on 'whether God could be best served within as opposed to outside the purview of society.'[173] He claims that 'during the seventeenth century ... [Baptists] remained a peculiar people, but their peculiarity was of a type that did not preclude a place in society,' see, for example, the person of William Kiffin, a Baptist, and a Member of Parliament, who also had access to the king. Freeman frames this as 'combin[ing] political quietism with a

---

[172] John Colwell, 'In Defence of Christendom', *Baptist Ministers' Journal* 298 (2007): 27-28.
[173] Bell, *Apocalypse How?*, 80. He sees evidence of this in the 1644 London Confession and the 1651 The Faith and Practice of Thirty Congregations.

slumbering radicalism that remained latently present in their faith and practice.'[174]

Chris Ellis argues in his study of Baptist worship that one of the four values or concerns he found present was an emphasis on the kingdom of God: 'its worship will look outwards to a human community which is broken and divided by sin and it will pray for that wider world and seek to be a sign of the Kingdom to the world through its own fellowship life and worship.'[175]

This position of dissent has been a no, a no to any sense of church and state being too closely aligned, where baptism and citizenship become synonymous, where the shape, time and content of worship is dictated by law, and where prestige and privileges are held by those in Christian ministry.[176] Baptists were carving out a space for the church to be the church in which their dissent was also a yes: a yes to the Lordship of Jesus, to the sovereignty of God over the conscience and to the local congregation as accountable to Christ directly.[177] It is the argument of Freeman that this tradition of dissent does not just remain in the past, but remains a living tradition. Baptists need to reclaim dissent as essential to their identity. 'Retelling the story of dissent' says Freeman, 'is a reminder that followers of Christ must learn to live in a perpetual

---

[174] Freeman, *Undomesticated Dissent*, 42.

[175] Ellis, *Gathering*, 229.

[176] So the classic criticisms of Helwys in *A Short Declaration*. See Introduction to *Protestant Nonconformist Texts, Vol.1* (Aldershot: Ashgate, 2007), 2.

[177] Michael R. Watts says something similar about the use of the description 'Free Church': 'it implies not merely rejection of the national church, it proposes a constructive alternative', *The Dissenters Vol.I* (Oxford: Clarendon, 1978), 2.

state of tension with the status quo, regardless of what it is'[178] because they live under the power of Christ into whom they have been baptised. A Baptist political theology will see the practice of the church meeting as a place where there is an ongoing conversation and discernment with Scripture, guided by the Holy Spirit on what it means to be baptised and to bear witness in the context of where the church finds itself. There is no blueprint, although the tradition of dissent does offer what Fiddes terms 'tracks.'[179] Freeman suggests the word to describe such reflection is 'conscience': 'to put it simply, conscience is a way of talking about how Christians in communion with one another exercise the mind of Christ (Phil 2.5).'[180] This position of dissent and concern for the kingdom gives a Baptist political theology an apocalyptic dimension that 'resist[s] accommodation to the way things are.' Freeman offers the following vision of a dissenting Christianity:

> Such communities grasp that seeing the world apocalyptically is not about predicting the future but about living in the light of the revelation that causes the world they inhabit to appear in an entirely new way. They promote the habits of an imagination that equips members with the capacity to see the world through the lens of the life, death, and resurrection of Jesus Christ. They read history backward, seeing their own lives retrospectively in continuity with the story of Israel's God and God's servant Jesus. They understand God's disruptive action in Christ not as a future event but as a reality that is always present and ever new. They do not withdraw into sectarian enclaves of homogeneity or accommodate to institutional structures of secularity but seek a life together that participates in the new

---

[178] Freeman, *Undomesticated Dissent*, 218.
[179] 'There are pathways trodden in the past which still have definite meaning and relevance for the present', Fiddes, *Tracks and Traces*, 1.
[180] Freeman, *Undomesticated Dissent*, 220.

creation and exemplifies what God in Christ intends for all humanity. They recognize that they do not bring God's reign in history but reach out to meet the new world that is on its way. They do not simply mirror the secular politics of left and right but seek to the practice the politics of Jesus through forgiveness and friendship. They refuse to regard distinctions of race, class, gender, or sexuality as determinative of standing in society but see only one new humanity in Christ. They seek the peace of the earthly city, telling the truth about what they see and advocating for the healing of its brokenness, but they recognize that their citizenship is in heaven. They see themselves as pilgrims in this secular age, answerable to the law of another city toward which they journey in faith on the wings of the love of God and neighbour.[181]

## Concluding Thoughts

Stanley Hauerwas writes that 'what we Christians have lost is just how radical our practices are.'[182] In this Whitley Lecture I have sought to reclaim some of the key practices that can be found among Baptists as radical[183] and political. The goal of this lecture has been modest, it has been to argue that Baptists are political by virtue of the convictions of our ecclesiology. Authority, liberty, administration, law, baptism, duty, and witness are political words; the church is a political body. By wanting to highlight how Baptists *are* a political theology, I have hopefully demonstrated that this is not one that maintains a strict separation of church and world. Baptists are those engaged in witness in the world and their posture of dissent is not world-denying, but

---

[181] Freeman, *Undomesticated Dissent*, 221-22.

[182] Stanley Hauerwas, *In Good Company: The Church as Polis* (Notre Dame, IN: University of Notre Dame, 1995), 8.

[183] 'Radical' is one of the words that Nigel Wright likes to use. See Goodliff, 'Nigel Wright's Radical Baptist Theology', 69-70.

critical of the state over-reaching itself. Newson drawing on McClendon describes the relationship of church to world as 'a dialectic' where 'the church is at times separate, at times open, entering into a rhythmic openness and closedness that operates in the same way as a healthy heart.'[184] Congregations cannot help but be in the world, the Declaration as we noted, defines a Baptist politic as one that 'take[s] part in the evangelization of the world.' The question becomes for a church on the way, which is being drawn into conversations and encounters, is thus, what is our witness?[185]

Our witness I suggest is one of a community under the rule of Christ, that submits to the authority of its Lord. It is a witness that requires an ongoing discernment of that rule for its life and mission, as it reads the scriptures and inhabits the world. It is a witness that lives from baptism, which gives us a new identity that transforms our other identities.[186] A baptised church is one that confronts the Powers in the world, acknowledging that the 'line between church and world passes right through each Christian heart.'[187] It is a witness that embodies and proclaims the Gospel of Jesus Christ not as those who have arrived, but as those who are always on the way. Elsewhere I have suggested that

---

[184] Newson, *Inhabiting the World*, 117, drawing on McClendon, *Witness*, 418-20.

[185] The phrasing of this question came out of the online meeting of the McClendon Reading Group on reading chapter one of McClendon's *Witness* volume, Monday 15th November 2021.

[186] See Hauerwas talk about being a Christian and a Texan (*Christian Existence Today* [Grand Rapids, MI: Brazos, 2001 [1988], 25-45), a Christian and an American (*A Better Hope* [Grand Rapids, MI: Brazos, 2000], 23-34).

[187] McClendon, *Ethics*, 17.

being Baptist is about participating in a conversation.[188] A Baptist political theology will see that conversation partners will not just be those in the church, but will include 'those not (yet) on the way.'[189] This reclaiming or recognising of our politics will always draw us into wider political, economic and social conversations. I end with two brief examples.[190]

First, one conversation that might be entered into is the relation of church and charity.[191] While churches are charitable, they are also more than charities. The 2006 UK Charities Act introduced a real tension for Baptists with regards to the imposition of trustees into a Baptist polity.[192] Colwell views it as 'corporate capitulation to a governmentally imposed Presbyterianism.'[193] Baptist churches have found themselves in an interesting situation, where we appreciate the financial rewards of being designated charities, but have found our life increasingly being legislated by the state.[194] As Julian Rivers says 'self

---

[188] Andy Goodliff, What Does it Mean to Be Baptist?', *Baptists Together* (Spring 2021), 10-11. At one point McClendon planned to give the title 'Conversations' to his third volume in his Systematic Theology, in the end he settled on *Witness*. There is though an overlapping link between the two.

[189] Curtis Freeman, 'Introduction' to James McClendon, *Systematic Theology Vol 1: Ethics* (Waco, TX: Baylor, 2012), xxix.

[190] A sequel to this lecture might engage more closely with the argument of Bretherton in *Christ and the Common Life*.

[191] A helpful overview can be found in Julian Rivers, *The Law of Organized Religions* (Oxford: Oxford University Press, 2010), 147-80.

[192] See Paul Fiddes and Graham Sparkes, 'Trusteeship: Theological Reflections'. Unpublished Paper presented to the Council of the Baptist Union, November 2005.

[193] Colwell, 'Integrity and Relatedness', 21.

[194] Ernest Payne raised this in 1952, see his *Free Churchmen, Unrepentant and Repentant* (London: Carey Kingsgate, 1965), 65-66. Ivan King explores this further in 'Degrees of Separation: An Exploration of Issues Arising from the Current Financial Relationship of UK Baptist Churches and the State', *Journal of European Baptist Studies* (Spring 2022).

regulation is giving way to compulsory Government regulation.'[195] The future implications are far from certain. A better sense of our dissenting history might require us to assess whether something of a Baptist understanding of how the rule of Christ is discerned has been lost and ask how it can be recovered.

Second, another conversation is to ask precisely what kind of discernment should churches engage in; what is appropriate to be the subject of a Church Meeting? It might be answered only 'matters relating to faith and practice', but what does not relate to faith and practice? Especially if our belief is that 'in Christ all things hold together' (Col 1.17). Stuart Blythe makes the case in a recent essay that Scottish churches should have put the question of Scottish independence on the agenda of their Church Meetings.[196] That this did not take place, he claims, 'represents a failure of discipleship.' His broader proposal is that Church Meetings 'should deal with the "matters that matter," including those of a socio-political nature.'[197] Blythe's argument flows from an understanding of the expansive nature of the Lordship of Christ and that the outcome of any discernment might be that in some issues, like those of a political nature, members are 'free to follow their conscience with our without any qualifying guidance of

---

[195] Rivers, *The Law of Organized Religions*, 161.

[196] Stuart Blythe, '"Your Will Be Always Done": Congregational Discernment as Contextual Discipleship' in *Gathering Disciples: Essays in Honor of Christopher J. Ellis* edited by Myra Blyth and Andy Goodliff (Eugene, OR: Pickwick, 2017), 74-88. See also his earlier, 'Engaging with Scottish Independence', *Baptist Times* 2 December 2013: https://www.baptist.org.uk/Articles/380926/Engaging_with_ Scottish.aspx. For another perspective see Steve Holmes, 'Communal Discernment and Church Meetings', 29 October 2014. http://steverholmes.org.uk/blog/?p=7358.

[197] Blythe, '"Your Will Be Always Done"', 78.

43

the congregation.'[198] The general point is that to avoid political questions is to suggest that discipleship is private and not a public matter.[199]

To address political and social issues in a Church Meeting would be a test of Baptist practices, which has potential to be good for our discipleship, as well as demonstrating that there is no matter that the gospel does not address.[200] For Christians to learn to listen and talk well on political matters in a Church Meeting is habit forming for listening and talking well in other gatherings, contributing to the common life of a local people and place.[201] It has the potential to show the difference that Christ makes and a way of seeking the kingdom, loving the neighbour, and bearing witness to the Gospel.[202]

---

[198] Blythe, "'Your Will Be Always Done'", 84.

[199] Blythe quotes from Glen Stassen, *A Thicker Jesus* (Louisville: WJK, 2012), 6 who suggests that to avoid any controversial issues is 'Enlightenment lite.'

[200] Anthony Clarke offers a way that Church Meetings might engage in this kind of theological reflection. See his 'Theological Reflections as Community Discernment: Some New Possibilities for Church Meetings' in *Being Attentive: Explorations in Practical Theology in Honour of Robert Ellis* edited by Anthony Clarke (Oxford: Regent's Park College, 2021), 156-74.

[201] In a forthcoming essay on ministry and geography I have attempted to show the importance of place.

[202] I am grateful to John Colwell, Ivan King, Ashley Lovett, and Sally Nelson for their comments on a draft of this lecture.

Printed in Great Britain
by Amazon